WELCOME

The Imperial War Museum was founded during the First World War to make sure that we never forget what it is like to live in a world torn apart by conflict.

Since then, IWM has spent a century recording the way in which war continues to impact on the lives of service personnel and civilians. From the fighting front and the home front, we have collected weapons, uniforms, vehicles, flags, maps, medals, films, audio recordings, photographs, diaries, letters, works of art and any other type of object that gives a sense of how war looks, sounds and feels.

There are stories to be told about every single one of these objects — stories about the people who owned them, used them or were affected by them; stories about how they were created or preserved; and wider stories about the nature of war itself. These stories can inspire, shock, inform, challenge, appal, surprise and move us; they can even change us.

Telling these stories is what IWM is all about. You will find thousands of them in our galleries and exhibitions — many displayed in spaces that we have regenerated and reshaped in the last few years to make them even more engaging. We hope you enjoy them.

CONTENTS

THE STORY OF IWM   4

ESSENTIAL IWM LONDON   6

WITNESSES TO WAR   8
Explore the museum's magnificent new atrium and discover the stories behind its eye-catching exhibits

FIRST WORLD WAR   10
Follow the story of the First World War, get to know some of the people who lived, fought and died in the conflict, and find out more about the exhibits

SECOND WORLD WAR   22
Explore clusters of specially chosen objects that provide revealing snapshots of the way that the Second World War was fought and experienced

PEACE AND SECURITY   38
Take a thought-provoking look at some of the most complex and controversial aspects of war from 1945 through to the present day

THE HOLOCAUST EXHIBITION   48
Place this powerful exhibition in context by reading a summary of how the Holocaust came about, and a timeline of its terrible chain of events

THE LORD ASHCROFT GALLERY   52
Celebrate the 'Extraordinary Heroes' whose bravery in the face of adversity has been recognised by the award of the Victoria Cross and George Cross

ART   56
Discover the amazing depth and breadth of the museum's art collection — ranging from paintings commissioned during the First World War to works reflecting current conflicts worldwide

EXPLORE FURTHER AND GET INVOLVED   60

IWM LONDON & YOU   62

ABOUT IMPERIAL WAR MUSEUMS   64

DID YOU KNOW?
The Latin inscription on the front of the museum building translates as 'Founded by King Henry VIII. Completed by the generosity of the people'. It refers to the hospital that once occupied the site.

ABOUT YOUR GUIDEBOOK

Your guidebook follows the layout of the museum, starting with the First World War Gallery on Level 0 and working up to the Lord Ashcroft Gallery on Level 5.

You can use it as a guide to your visit on the day, and as a souvenir afterwards, when you can enjoy the different perspective that it gives to the exhibitions and displays.

Narrative
Simple summary of the exhibition's story

Objects in depth
Key objects explained from different angles

Key exhibits
Important exhibits captured in photographs and highlighted in **bold** in the text

People
Stories of people connected to the exhibits

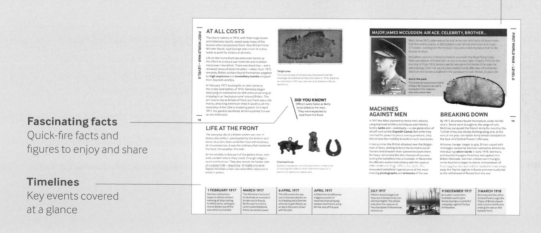

Fascinating facts
Quick-fire facts and figures to enjoy and share

Timelines
Key events covered at a glance

Original layout
A view of the museum's army section display at the Crystal Palace in 1920.
IWM Q 31438

IWM TIMELINE
On 5 March 1917, the War Cabinet approved a proposal for the creation of a National War Museum to record the events still taking place in the First World War. Interest among the Dominion governments soon led to it being re-named the Imperial War Museum.

9 JUNE 1920
The museum is opened at the Crystal Palace by King George V. In 1924 it moves to a location in South Kensington.

7 JULY 1936
The Duke of York, soon to become King George VI, re-opens the museum at its present home on Lambeth Road, South London

THE STORY OF IWM

The Imperial War Museum was established in 1917 even as the First World War was still being fought. From the very beginning its purpose was to record warfare as it was experienced by individuals. Service personnel and civilians, men and women, rich and poor – it would commemorate the effort and sacrifices made by all.

The museum has had three homes – the Crystal Palace for four years, South Kensington for eleven, and then its current site in Lambeth since 1936. The building that it occupies today used to be the central portion of Bethlem Royal Hospital, or 'Bedlam' – a place of treatment for the mentally ill that can trace its history back, via numerous London locations, to 1247.

Over the course of more than 75 years, the IWM London building has been expanded to create more archive and exhibition space. And in the run-up to the First World War Centenary, the site was transformed again to create the magnificent new atrium space and an improved experience for all our visitors.

DID YOU KNOW?

Britain's army was so short of equipment after Dunkirk in 1940 that 18 of IWM's artillery pieces were returned to military service.

Museum unveiled
A poster advertises the opening of the Imperial War Museum at the Crystal Palace in South London.
IWM PST 3278

AUGUST 1939
IWM begins moving its collections away from London, and closes from 1940 to 1946. Its remit is also expanded to include the Second World War.

MARCH 1953
The Korean War prompts another redefinition of IWM – to cover all conflicts since 1914 involving Britain or the Commonwealth

1970s – 2000s
Four new branches are opened – IWM Duxford in 1976, HMS *Belfast* in 1978, the Cabinet (now Churchill) War Rooms in 1984, and IWM North in 2002

JULY 2014
IWM London re-opens after a major re-development designed to commemorate the Centenary of the First World War

ESSENTIAL IWM LONDON

Every object on display at IWM London has the power to grip, move and inspire. It could be something small like a **lucky charm** carried by a British soldier in the trenches, or something much bigger like the **atomic bomb** casing displayed at the heart of the museum. Here are just a few items and experiences to look out for on your way round.

EXPERIENCE THE TRENCHES

As you explore the **First World War Galleries** on **Level 0**, look out for the **Life at the Front** area. Here you can experience for yourself some of the sights and sounds that were part of daily life for those on the Western Front.

The Mule Track

Also in the **First World War Galleries**, see this famous painting by Paul Nash. Amidst the smoke and fire of a heavy bombardment, the tiny figures of a mule train are trying to cross the bleak landscape of the battlefield.
IWM ART 1153

GET CURIOUS

Be sure to explore **Curiosities of War** – the intriguing section of the museum where you will find all manner of unlikely objects, including a **Playstation**, a **hotel bar** and a **full-size wooden horse** (left). Go to **Level 3** to find out more.

IWM FEQ 935

CATCH THE LATEST EXHIBITIONS

Head to **Level 3** and you'll find an innovative programme of special exhibitions that explore multiple perspectives on the impact of conflict on people's lives. A programme of live events accompanies these exhibitions, offering visitors a unique opportunity to meet and take part in discussions with those who have lived through conflict.

DID YOU KNOW?

The naval guns outside IWM London were fired in action during the Second World War. One is from HMS *Ramillies*, the other from HMS *Resolution*.

MEET A PRIME MINISTER

Go eye-to-eye with former Prime Minister Margaret Thatcher — or at least the iconic puppet of her (below) famously created for satirical TV show *Spitting Image*. You'll find her waiting in **Peace and Security** on **Level 2**.

IWM EPH 9800

GO INTERACTIVE

Use the **Supply Line** table on **Level 0** to keep Britain's First World War troops fed and fighting; and use the **touchscreen displays** in the **Lord Ashcroft Gallery** on **Level 5** to uncover animated illustrated stories about acts of extraordinary bravery.

IWM COM 228

AND DON'T MISS

- The nose of a Lancaster bomber, with its 49 circles on the side recording every misson it flew from November 1943 to March 1944

- The eye-popping display of camouflaged **model ships** in the **museum café** on **Level 0**

- The mangled **World Trade Center window frame** from the terrorist attack of 11 September 2001 in **Peace and Security** on **Level 2**

WITNESSES TO WAR

Enter the museum's magnificent Atrium and you are met with an array of objects that bear witness to the force, fury and physicality of war. Each has a story to tell – from the **First World War artillery piece** that became a memorial for the men who fought with it, to the wreckage of the **Land Rover** operated on the Gaza Strip by the press agency Reuters. Here are five others that you simply must not miss.

Baghdad car (right)

This car was destroyed in a suicide car bombing at a historic book market in Baghdad in March 2007. The blast killed dozens of people at a time of rising sectarian violence in Iraq.

IWM 4907.20.1

Spitfire (above)

The fighter plane on display flew 57 combat missions during the Battle of Britain in 1940. It was flown by 13 different pilots, only 6 of whom survived the Second World War.

IWM SITE LAM 00103_1

V2 rocket (right)

From September 1944, Germany deployed the V2 rocket against London and other cities in Europe. A rocket like the one on display struck the nearby Kennington Road/ Lambeth Road crossroads on 4 January 1945, killing 43 people.

IWM MUN 3853

Harrier Jet (above)

This British ground attack aircraft flew patrols over northern Iraq in the early 1990s and was twice deployed to Afghanistan. It was once sat in by David Cameron during a visit to Afghanistan in 2006 – a few years before he became Prime Minister.

DID YOU KNOW?

Wernher von Braun, the German engineer behind the V2 rocket, went on to play a key role in the United States' space programme that ultimately landed a man on the Moon.

T-34 tank (right)

Tanks like this Soviet-designed T-34 played such a key role in the Second World War that they became symbolic of the Soviet war effort and were often used as war memorials. This particular tank was built in 1954 and later sold to the Egyptian Army. It was captured by the Israelis in 1973.

IWM 4800.60.2

FIRST WORLD WAR

The **First World War Galleries** tell the story of how the 'Great War' was fought and won, its impact on people's lives on the front and at home, and its far-reaching consequences. They begin with a look at the years leading up to the conflict.

Few anticipated that the summer of 1914 would end with war in Europe. There had been no general European war for almost 100 years, during which a delicate balance of power had been maintained between Europe's leading nations. But all this began to change with the dramatic rise of Germany following its unification in 1871.

Russia and France, alarmed by Germany's growing strength, formed an alliance. Germany, now threatened from east and west, drew closer to its ally Austria-Hungary. Britain was allied to no-one, but to secure its Empire, it reached agreements with its traditional rivals, France and Russia. Diplomatic incidents peppered the early years of the twentieth century, but always fell short of war. As a result Britain began to see it as essential to support France against its more powerful neighbour Germany.

DID YOU KNOW?

The First World War has been called the ultimate family feud. Britain's King George V, Germany's Kaiser Wilhelm II and Russia's Tsar Nicholas II were all first cousins.

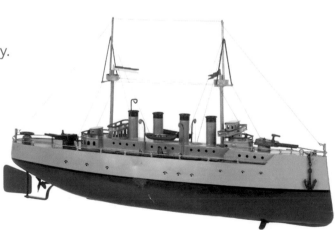

Faces of war

A group of men from the Oxford and Buckinghamshire Light Infantry shelter from shrapnel behind the headquarters of 20 Brigade, Ypres, 1914.

IWM Q 57205

Growing rivalry

By 1914, a toy battleship was a popular purchase for patriotic German parents, keen to show pride in the fleet being built to rival Britain's Royal Navy.

IWM EPH 2937

WILLIAM WILLIAMS: BACKBONE OF THE ARMY

Company Sergeant Major William Williams hailed from Bolton, Lancashire and joined The Worcestershire Regiment in January 1896 at the age of 19. By the time of the First World War, he had spent almost half his life serving in South Africa, Ceylon (modern-day Sri Lanka) and India. It was men like Williams – all 5 foot 5½ inches of him – who formed the backbone of the British Army.

On 31 October 1914 the Germans launched an attack near the strategically important Belgian town of Ypres. Williams was fatally wounded during a charge that forced the enemy to retreat. A fighter to the end, he did not succumb to his wounds until 8 November.

Career soldier

This tunic belonged to Company Sergeant Major William Williams. He was the type of experienced soldier that the British Army could ill afford to lose.

IWM UNI 12214

WHY WAR?

On 28 June 1914, Archduke Franz Ferdinand, heir to the Austro-Hungarian throne, was assassinated by a Serbian-backed terrorist. Austria-Hungary looked to punish its troublesome neighbour, Serbia, stirring old tensions and drawing in allies on both sides. Germany supported Austria-Hungary, its only reliable ally. Russia backed Serbia.

On 28 July Austria-Hungary declared war on Serbia, prompting the members of the two rival power blocs to prepare their armies. Aiming for a quick victory against France before Russia's huge army could intervene, Germany declared war on both. The British agonised over what to do but came to a decision when Germany invaded Belgium to get to France. Germany was ignoring a treaty under which it and Britain guaranteed Belgium's neutrality. On 4 August Britain too declared war.

SHOCK

Generals, soldiers, politicians and civilians quickly discovered that this war was going to be like nothing the world had seen before. Soldiers on all sides, sometimes marching forward in their traditional **colourful uniforms** and equipped with lances and swords, were met with the power and accuracy of modern artillery fire – provided by the likes of the **French 75mm quickfiring field gun**. Britain's small professional army was all but destroyed.

By the end of the year, exhausted soldiers were seeking refuge in trenches. The war was undecided, and the terrible losses during 1914 meant that there could be no swift end to it. Few could now imagine peace without a victory to show for the sacrifices made.

Misplaced confidence

This German medallion was made in anticipation of a speedy victory march into Paris. Such high hopes were quickly proved false on all sides.

IWM EPH 10155

FIRST WORLD WAR TIMELINE

When war broke out in 1914, neither side expected it to go on for four years and cost the lives of some ten million servicemen. This timeline shows the main events of those four years – the quick descent into deadlock, the attempts to break it, and the eventual and sudden end.

28 JULY 1914

A month after the heir to the Austro-Hungarian throne is assassinated by a Bosnian terrorist, Austria-Hungary declares war on Serbia

4 AUGUST 1914

After agonising over whether to support its friend France, Britain declares war on Germany when the latter invades neutral Belgium

Call to arms
The newly-created Parliamentary Recruiting Committee produced 12.5 million posters in 160 different designs calling for volunteers to join the British Army.
IWM PST 5086, IWM PST 11363, IWM PST 11407

YOUR COUNTRY NEEDS YOU

As soon as the war began, Lord Kitchener, the new war minister, launched an appeal for 100,000 volunteers to swell the ranks of Britain's Army. By the end of September he had 750,000. Some simply wanted to escape the drudgery of urban life or to secure paid work; others were outraged by **reports of German atrocities** in Belgium or felt the lure of an adventure on foreign fields. The call was answered with similar enthusiasm across Britain's Empire.

Civilians unable to join the Army needed little persuasion to contribute to the cause, buying paper flags to raise funds for the war effort or sending comforts to troops on the front — like the **Christmas pudding** and **tin of sweets** on display in the Galleries. They also showed their support for the war by their enthusiastic consumption of violent anti-German propaganda.

DID YOU KNOW?

Nine-year-old Alfie Knight wrote a letter to Lord Kitchener, volunteering his services as a frontline bicycle messenger. His offer was turned down in an official reply from the War Office. Both the letter and the reply are on display in the Galleries.

AUGUST – SEPTEMBER 1914

Germany crushes a Russian advance at the Battles of Tannenberg and the Masurian Lakes in East Prussia (part of modern-day Poland)

SEPTEMBER 1914

French and British troops halt the Germans at the Battle of the Marne (right), close to Paris
IWM Q 51489

OCTOBER 1914

Turkey joins with Germany and Austria-Hungary against the Allies

DEADLOCK

In the open warfare of 1914, men on both sides had quickly taken to scraping holes in the ground to shelter from artillery fire. By the end of December, these scrapes had evolved into a network of trenches, with each side camped opposite the other. It was the only sensible way to slow down the appalling casualty rate.

As the occupying force, the Germans could afford to sit tight and gradually wear out their enemies. It was up to the British and French to drive the Germans out. In 1915 this amounted to periodic, costly advances across the no man's land between the two trench systems.

For both sides, trench warfare was an unfamiliar challenge, which led to the development of new weapons such as the **Stokes trench mortar** and the refinement of others such as the **Mills bomb** grenade. Some ancient arts were also revived, such as digging tunnels to lay explosives under enemy lines.

14

For every measure there came a counter-measure. When the Germans used poison gas at Ypres in April 1915, for example, the British were quick to follow suit and both sides developed all manner of **respirators**, **protective gear** and **warning gongs, rattles and horns**. Gas was not to be a war-winning weapon and the year ended as it began – in stalemate.

Colonial combat
Thousands of Africans fought for the colonial powers. This fez was worn by an 'Askari', an African soldier serving with German colonial forces in Cameroon.
IWM UNI 12450

WORLD WAR

From the outset this was a war of empires – a true world war with battlefields spread across continents and oceans. On the seas, each side tried to sever the other's supply lines, the British by mounting a blockade, the Germans by targeting merchant ships with submarines. On land, new fronts were opened and new allies sought, as the warring powers looked to win the war away from the deadlocked Western Front.

Turkey came in on the side of the Central Powers and launched a botched attack on Russia. Britain planned to knock Turkey out of the war by bombarding its capital from the sea. But troops – including men from Australia, New Zealand, Canada, India, France and Britain – had to be landed when the way was barred by Turkish forces on the Gallipoli peninsula. A trench-bound deadlock resembling the Western Front ensued – with a humiliating British evacuation the ultimate outcome.

The USA was angered by the naval blockades mounted by Britain and Germany, which hampered neutral shipping. When German submarines began to sink ships, including the ocean liner *Lusitania*, without warning, this anger became focused on Germany. Germany was forced to rein in its submarines for fear of bringing the USA into the war.

Close quarter fighting
In trench warfare, clubs and knives were as vital to a soldier as his gun – a throwback to more primitive eras of warfare.
IWM WEA 3069

FEEDING THE FRONT

In 1915 voluntary recruiting in Britain was in decline and industry could not keep up with the Army's demand for munitions. The government looked to rally Britain's resources. A new Ministry of Munitions took control of war production. Huge new factories were created, and made as much use as possible of workers not needed by the Army – the old, the very young and women. Women had always formed a significant part of Britain's working population; now they turned their hands to war work.

The Army recruitment shortfall brought about an even more radical change to British society. In early 1916, after months of furious debate, conscription was introduced. All men aged 18 to 41 were eventually made liable for service. Britain's men could no longer choose whether or not to fight.

Badge of honour
Employers issued 'On War Service' badges to show that their workers were not shirking military service, but undertaking vital war work.
IWM INS 7767

DID YOU KNOW?

From October 1915 onwards it was illegal in Britain to treat other people to a round of drinks. Too much alcohol was thought to be damaging to productivity.

GABRIELLE WEST: WORKER, POLICE OFFICER, GROUND-BREAKER...

In the year from June 1915 some 563,000 women began working in war industries. Inside the workplace they had to adhere to a strict set of rules. Outside, they were a highly visible presence in the houses, schools, shops and cinemas that sprang up around the new factories.

One of these women was Gabrielle West, whose wartime **diaries** are displayed in the Galleries. In late 1916, after stints in the kitchen of a Red Cross hospital and the canteens of various munitions factories, West joined the newly created Women's Police Force – set up to supervise the female workers. By the time of her last diary entry in May 1917, she was a sergeant working at the Hereford Shell Factory.

Force for change
Gabrielle West is thought to be one of the Women Police Officers posing in this photograph. Such a Police Force was unthinkable before the war.
DOCUMENTS.7142

DECEMBER 1914
Two opposing lines of trenches stretch from the Belgian coast to Switzerland, forming the Western Front

FEBRUARY 1915
The Allies launch a naval assault on Turkey. Troops are later landed at Gallipoli (right), but the campaign ends in failure in 1916.
IWM Q 13622

MAY 1915
Hoping to knock Russia out of the war, Germany begins a series of successful offensives in the East. But Russia proves too strong to defeat in a single campaign.

TOTAL WAR

Both sides had high hopes for 1916. The British and French planned a series of massive coordinated attacks to wear down – and perhaps even break – the German front line.

The main attack was to fall at the junction of the British and French armies in Picardy – on the River Somme – but the plans had to change when the Germans launched their own surprise offensive at Verdun. French troops had to pour in to mount a defence, leaving the British as the major Allied force at the Somme. The new British civilian army would be going into battle en masse for the first time.

The offensive began with a long bombardment of the German lines by heavy artillery such as the **9.2-inch howitzer**. It was hoped that this would allow a mass infantry advance across no man's land – through breached barbed wire defences and facing much reduced artillery and automatic fire from the likes of the **German MG 08 machine gun**.

But the bombardment provided for by the British **artillery plan** was not concentrated enough, and 30 per cent of the heavy shells were duds. The scene was set for a slaughter. From 7.30am on 1 July 1916, around 100,000 British troops went 'over the top'. By the end of the day 20,000 were dead. It was the single most costly day in the history of the British Army.

World at war
Troops of the British West Indies Regiment are pictured behind the lines near the Somme battlefield in September 1916. Over 16,000 men from the West Indies served in the First World War.
IWM Q 1202

For almost five months the British and French made repeated attacks on the Somme Front – in midsummer heat and autumnal mud. With their allies fighting hard on other fronts, they had to continue with their part of the grand Allied plan.

In the context of the war, their efforts were not in vain. The Germans were dismayed at the seemingly limitless supply of men and munitions hurled against them. The Allies may have lost 600,000 men – killed, wounded, missing or captured – but the Germans lost 500,000 of their own, soaking up their reserves and sealing the failure of their Verdun offensive.

Despite the heavy losses of the Somme, the British Army gained confidence that it could match the Germans in large-scale battles. Germany's leaders, meanwhile, feared subjecting their men to a similar ordeal. Their determination to avoid 'another Somme' was to have fateful effects on their decision-making for the remainder of the war.

DID YOU KNOW?

The documentary film 'The Battle of the Somme' was seen by 20 million people in Britain in late 1916. It is also shown in the Galleries.

21 FEBRUARY 1916
The Germans attack the fortress of Verdun, hoping to force France out of the war. But the French Army holds firm.

31 MAY 1916
The British and German fleets clash in the Battle of Jutland (right). The battle is indecisive but the Germans do not venture out again.
IWM SP 2156

1 JULY 1916
Allied troops attack on the Somme – the most costly day of the war for the British Army. A bitter struggle continues into November.

BRITISH 9.2-INCH HOWITZER

The opening bombardment of the Somme offensive involved over 1,400 artillery pieces, including 88 borrowed from the French and 20 converted naval guns.

The 9.2-inch howitzer on display in the Galleries was capable of firing its 132-kilogram shells at targets some 10 kilometres away, and its high angle of fire made it ideally suited to the siege-like conditions of the Western Front.

In addition to bombarding enemy defences, it was often used to conduct so-called 'counter-battery' fire – targeting German artillery positions.

It took a crew of 14 to operate the 9.2-inch howitzer – hot work in the summer months of the Battle of the Somme.

The gun had to be fired from a fixed position on a platform set into the ground. To counterbalance the recoil effect of the howitzer's 12-tonne weight, a box filled with tonnes of earth had to be attached to the front of the mount.

"MOTHER"

Lieutenant Adrian Consett Stephen wrote about the howitzer gun in a letter dated July 1916.

'My Lord the gun! ...His snout tilts upward, sniffing the air, his lips slobber with smoke and flame. All night men sleep around him, and further behind the line an army toil to feed him with long rows of glistening shells. Men and gun are one and indivisible. My Lord the Gun has come into his own, and his kingdom today is large – it is the world.'

'My Lord the Gun has come into his own...'

This particular howitzer was known as 'Mother'. It was a prototype – the only gun of its kind when it arrived at the Western Front in October 1914. Volume production did not get underway until the following year, and the British Army only had 60 at its disposal during the Somme bombardment.

Heavy artillery of this type – including even more powerful 12-inch and 15-inch howitzers – eventually proved to be the key to victory on the Western Front. However, it wasn't until 1917 that Britain had enough heavy guns and shells to tip the balance of war in its favour.

AT ALL COSTS

The titanic battles of 1916, with their huge losses and indecisive results, swept away many of the leaders who had planned them. New British Prime Minister David Lloyd George was a man of action, ready to push for victory at all costs.

Life on the home front became even harder as the effort to produce war materials and mobilise manpower intensified. There was shock too – and a renewed sense of determination – when, from 1915 onwards, British civilians found themselves targeted by **high explosive** and **incendiary bombs** dropped from Zeppelin airships.

In February 1917, looking for an alternative to the costly land battles of 1916, Germany began deploying its submarines to sink without warning all shipping in an 'exclusion zone' around Britain. The aim was to starve Britain of food, but there was a risk that by attacking American ships it would push the neutrality of the USA to breaking point. On 6 April 1917, the gamble backfired; America joined the war on the Allied side.

Target area
This charred map of London was recovered from the wreckage of a German airship shot down in 1916. Wartime air raids killed 1,413 men, women and children in Britain.
IWM EPH 2212

DID YOU KNOW?
Officers were twice as likely to be killed as the men. They were expected to lead from the front.

LIFE AT THE FRONT

The everyday life of a British soldier was one of dreary discomfort, punctuated by the tension and terror of action. Even amid the most extraordinary of circumstances, it was the ordinary that mattered: the food, the weather, the mail.

As the exhibits in this part of the gallery show, men took comfort where they could, through religion, sport and humour. They also reveal the harder side of a soldier's life – discipline, ill health and what happened when a man was wounded, captured or killed in action.

Charmed lives
Soldiers sometimes carried lucky charms in the hope of avoiding the bullet or shell 'with their name on it'.
IWM EPH 3473, IWM EPH 3475, IWM EPH 4896

1 FEBRUARY 1917	**MARCH 1917**	**6 APRIL 1917**	**APRIL 1917**
German submarines begin to attack without warning all ships sailing to Allied ports, aiming to starve Britain out of the war within six months	Tsar Nicholas II is forced to abdicate as revolution breaks out in Russia. By the year's end the communist Bolshevik Party has seized power.	The USA enters the war, due to German attacks on its shipping and a German attempt to gain Mexico as an ally in the event of war with the USA	A failed French offensive triggers a series of mutinies that seriously weaken the French army for the rest of the year

MAJOR JAMES MCCUDDEN: AIR ACE, CELEBRITY, BROTHER...

Major James McCudden was an 'air ace': an airman who had shot down more than five enemy planes. In McCudden's case, he had shot down a lot more – 57 in total – earning him the Victoria Cross and a celebrity status that he did his best to shun.

McCudden was one of three brothers to serve with the Royal Flying Corps. Willie was killed in 1915 and John, an ace in his own right, in March 1918. On the morning of 9 July 1918, James is said to have given his medals to his sister for safe-keeping. Later that day his plane stalled shortly after take-off and James died from the injuries sustained in the subsequent crash. He was 23 years old.

Ace in the pack
The shattered windscreen (right) of Major McCudden's aircraft is displayed in the Galleries.
IWM Q 67600, IWM EPH 9003

MACHINES AGAINST MEN

In 1917 the Allies planned to renew their attacks, using improved artillery techniques and infantry tactics, **tanks** and – eventually – a new generation of aircraft such as the **Sopwith Camel**. But while they now had the power to pierce enemy positions, they did not have the mobility to build on such successes.

In late summer the British attacked near the Belgian town of Ypres, aiming to force the Germans out of Flanders and threaten their submarine bases there. But heavy rain ended the slim chances of success, turning the battlefield into a mudbath. In November the offensive ended indecisively with the capture of the shattered village of Passchendaele. The devastated battlefield inspired some of the most enduring **photographs** and **artworks** of the war.

BREAKING DOWN

19

By 1917 all armies found themselves under terrific strain. Some were brought to the verge of ruin. Mutinies paralysed the French Army for months; the Turkish Army was slowly disintegrating and, at the end of the year, the Italian Army almost collapsed in the face of a Central Powers' offensive.

At home, hunger began to grip. Britain coped with shortages caused by German submarine attacks by introducing **ration cards** in early 1918. Germany and Austria-Hungary fared less well against the British blockade. German civilians went hungry; some Austrians began to starve. A breakdown of food supplies also sparked the revolution that swept away the Tsarist regime in Russia and eventually led to the withdrawal of Russia from the war.

JULY 1917
A British assault begins at Ypres but is hindered by rain and mud (right). The attack ends after the capture of Passchendaele in November.
IWM E(AUS) 1220

9 DECEMBER 1917
Jerusalem surrenders to British and Empire forces during a successful campaign against Turkey in Palestine.

3 MARCH 1918
Germany and the other Central Powers sign the Treaty of Brest-Litovsk with communist Russia ending the war on the Eastern Front

SEIZING VICTORY

In spring 1918 Germany launched a huge offensive on the Western Front — gambling on winning the war before the US Army was ready to fight. German advances made the Allied leaders fear defeat. But they did not let the crisis divide them. Maintaining their unity, the Allies held on until the Germans had exhausted themselves in repeated attacks. Then, in July, they began to counter-attack.

Soon they pushed the Germans out of all the territory they had seized in 1918. In September the US Army began to fight as an independent force for the first time. At the beginning of October, British and Empire forces broke through the main German line of the defence. It was one of the most clear-cut victories of the war.

Germany now asked for an armistice — a ceasefire to give its army respite from the repeated Allied attacks. Meanwhile its allies began to negotiate armistices of their own; with Bulgaria, Turkey and, eventually, Austria-Hungary all surrendering. In Germany revolution threatened and the Kaiser was forced to abdicate. With defeats continuing at the front and with the country in chaos, Germany's new government had to accept whatever conditions the Allies offered. The **terms of the Armistice** which brought the fighting to an end, on 11 November 1918, constituted a humiliating surrender.

WAR WITHOUT END

In 1919 the victorious Allies met in Paris to agree a peace settlement — its signing captured in a **painting by William Orpen** for IWM. Germany was stripped of its military power, forced to give up territory and ordered to pay financial reparations. The peacemakers confirmed the creation of new nations from the ashes of the Austro-Hungarian, Turkish and Russian Empires. Few were fully satisfied with the peace terms, but hope lay with the League of Nations — a new organisation intended to prevent wars.

In Britain, the war weakened social barriers but also encouraged greater government intervention in everyday life. In 1918 the country became more democratic when the right to vote was extended to most men and, for the first time, to women. A **leaflet** had to be produced to advise first-time voters how to exercise their new right. The British Empire grew, as Britain gained control of former Turkish and German colonies. But closer to home, the wartime growth of nationalism in Ireland erupted into guerrilla warfare which, in 1921, brought the partition of the country into a southern Free State and Northern Ireland.

The world had become more unstable. Away from Western Europe, fighting continued into the 1920s in many regions. Extreme political movements were on the rise. But this did not make another war inevitable. People attending the opening of IWM in June 1920 had reason to share the hope expressed in a speech by King George V that it was now possible to 'look back on war, its instruments, and its organisation, as belonging to a dead past'.

We will remember them
The first poppy appeal took place in 1921 — a form of remembrance that remains with us to this day.
IWM EPH 2313

---

21 MARCH 1918
Germany launches a Spring Offensive (right). Weathering the storm, the Allies counter successfully from July.
IWM Q 55020

SEPTEMBER 1918
British Empire forces rout the Turkish Army in Palestine. The surrender of Bulgaria exposes Constantinople to attack. Defeat looms for Turkey.

NOVEMBER 1918
Defeats force Germany to request an armistice, on 4 October 1918. But the fighting continues until the armistice agreement is signed on 11 November.

Peace at last
Airmen, soldiers and civilians
gather in Birmingham to celebrate
Armistice Day, 11 November 1918.
IWM Q 63690

SECOND WORLD WAR

Turning Points: 1934 to 1945 focuses on the Second World War – using groups of objects to deliver a series of insights about the way the war changed the world. It tells the story not of the war itself but of individual objects – and the people and events connected to them. It starts with the run-up to war.

The scars of the First World War were keenly felt across 1930s Europe – in its fractured political and economic landscape, and in the hearts of the many millions who had lost loved ones.

The peace settlement signed at Versailles in 1919 had been intended to prevent Germany from ever again being able to mount a military threat to the continent. And yet, just 15 years later, the country had a defiant new dictator in Adolf Hitler, whose hypnotic hold over Germany was captured vividly by film director Leni Riefenstahl's **Triumph of the Will** – as you can see for yourself in the displays.

DID YOU KNOW?
In 1941 the British Ministry of Information funded a short spoof of 'Triumph of the Will', editing footage from the film to make it appear as if Hitler and his SS men were marching and dancing to the song 'The Lambeth Walk'.

Ascent to power
Adolf Hitler climbs to the speaker's podium during the 1934 Harvest Thanksgiving Ceremony at Bückeberg. His aggressive policies would lead to war before the end of the decade.
IWM MH 11040

Lost property
Jewish couple Leonhard and Clara Wöhl sent their belongings out of Germany in this trunk during the summer of 1939. The outbreak of war meant that they could not follow it. They died in Auschwitz.
IWM EPH 2472

WAR ON THE WAY

As they watched Hitler rebuilding Germany's armed forces and beginning to intimidate neighbouring states, politicians and civilians across the world feared that a new war was coming – but hoped that it might still be avoidable.

Governments and individuals made preparations for war, from the development of better technology such as the powerful **Merlin engine** designed by Rolls-Royce for Britain's fighter and bomber aircraft, to the desperate attempts by German Jews such as the **Wöhl family** to escape overseas before war made such travel impossible.

Even after Prime Minister Neville Chamberlain extracted an **agreement with Hitler** in September 1938 to pursue diplomatic rather than military solutions, few were surprised when war came twelve months later.

In Britain, the popular cartoon character **Old Bill** captured the public mood: people didn't want to fight, but they could see the need for it, and they knew it was just a matter of time.

Fire fighter

A helmet worn by a member of the Fire Guard, set up in 1941 to incorporate smaller groups such as the Fire Watchers and Street Fire Parties hurriedly created to cope with the German bombing raids of 1940.
IWM UNI 509

MINDSET

After the catastrophic experience of the First World War, people feared the worst as units of the British Expeditionary Force (BEF) headed across the English Channel to take up positions with the French on the Maginot Line.

However, there was no significant confrontation on the Western Front in the first few months of the war. That all changed on 10 May 1940 when the Germans launched a sudden offensive. A few shocking days later they had burst their way through the Allied lines.

Within two weeks, the BEF was being evacuated from the coastline around the French port of Dunkirk. A makeshift fleet of ships and small boats, including the 15-foot *Tamzine*, ferried men to larger warships moored away from the shore.

Britain was now under threat of invasion and **secret maps** show how the German army intended to land and advance on London. First, though, Hitler needed to establish air superiority over southern

DID YOU KNOW?

Twenty months after invading Poland in September 1939, Germany had also conquered Denmark, Luxembourg, Holland, Belgium, Norway, France, Yugoslavia and Greece.

SECOND WORLD WAR TIMELINE

Fighting in the Second World War ranged far and wide, from the Arctic to the Pacific, North-West Europe to the Soviet Union, North Africa to the Far East. It lasted almost six years, claiming the lives of some 55 million men, women and children.

1 SEPTEMBER 1939

Germany invades Poland. Two days later, Britain, France, Australia and New Zealand all declare war.

10 MAY 1940

Hitler launches a devastating offensive in the West. Six weeks later the French are forced to surrender.

HAROLD NEWGASS GC: BOMB DISPOSAL HERO

On 28 November 1940 a German **parachute mine** fell on to the Garston Gasworks in Merseyside and came to rest, unexploded. To defuse it, someone would have to climb down to the floor of a pitch-black gas holder, wade through thick coal tar sludge, and use breathing apparatus to cope with the highly flammable, noxious fumes. Worse still, time was short because the local fire service could only provide six cylinders of oxygen, each lasting just 30 minutes. The odds were stacked against him but 41-year-old Harold Newgass, with all of two months' experience behind him, completed the job.

Decorated for bravery

Harold Newgass earned the George Cross for managing to defuse a parachute mine (right).
TRINITY MIRROR/LIVERPOOL ECHO, IWM MUN 3509

England and so began the Battle of Britain in July 1940. Fighter planes such as the British **Spitfire** and the German Messerschmitt Bf-109 engaged in dramatic dogfights throughout the hot months of summer, with the British gradually gaining the ascendancy by September.

Meanwhile, there came a new threat from the skies, as British cities – and civilians – became the target for a campaign of bombing raids known as the Blitz. The war had already become part of everyday life for Britons, with men, women and children all taking up new duties or daily routines, and items such as the Anderson Shelter, **Morrison Shelter, helmets** and **armbands** becoming commonplace. People knew that Britain was fighting for its survival.

Bedtime

The steel Morrison Shelter was introduced in Britain in 1941. Designed to be used in the home, it was big enough to sleep two adults and one child – and also doubled as a table.
IWM MOD 394

4 JUNE 1940

The evacuation from Dunkirk ends. Some 250,000 British troops are rescued (right), allowing Britain to keep fighting.
IWM H 1623

10 JUNE 1940

Italy enters the war on Germany's side and in September invades Egypt from Libya

JULY 1940

The Battle of Britain begins, as the Luftwaffe vies unsuccessfully with the Royal Air Force for control of the skies over southern England

LIFEBLOOD

After the fall of France, Britons were more grateful than ever for the natural defence provided by the sea. The oceans had been vital to the war effort since the first days of the war, when the Royal Navy effectively closed off the seas around Germany. Ships entering the area were stopped and searched and **contraband goods** were confiscated to put a stranglehold on the enemy's economy.

As an island, Britain was much more reliant on the seas than Germany; the flow of maritime trade was the country's lifeblood. If Germany could threaten those supply lines – especially in the Atlantic – there would be no need for an invasion; starved of oil, food, ships and weapons, Britain would be brought to its knees.

Every time ships like the **SS *San Demetrio*** took to sea, they faced danger from above and especially below the waves. By 1941, the Germans could put some 80 submarines into the Atlantic at any one time, with the **Type VIIC U-boat** to the fore. Their most feared weapon was the torpedo, especially the **Type G7e T3** introduced in 1942, which left no wake to be spotted even by the keenest-eyed look-out.

What helped to turn the 'Battle of the Atlantic' in Britain's favour was the breaking of the signals encoded and sent via **Enigma machines** to and from Germany's U-boats. By combining this intelligence with new tactics and technology, the Royal Navy could provide adequate protection for the convoys of merchant ships.

Hidden danger
This Type G7e T3 torpedo could strike without warning. Powered by an electric motor rather than compressed air, it left no visible trail of bubbles in the water.
IWM MUN 3847

DID YOU KNOW?
Only one thing ever really scared Prime Minister Winston Churchill during the war. He called it the 'U-boat peril' and he thought it might spell defeat for Britain.

Shipbuilding on the Clyde
A detail from a wartime painting by artist Stanley Spencer, commissioned to record the huge effort required to replace ships lost at sea.
IWM ART LD 3106

SEPTEMBER 1940	FEBRUARY 1941	22 JUNE 1941	7 DECEMBER 1941
Germany subjects Britain to the 'Blitz' – nine months of bombing raids on cities and towns designed to force Britain to surrender	German troops arrive in North Africa to reinforce the Italians, who have been forced back into Libya by British troops	After conquering Yugoslavia, Greece and Crete in April and May, Germany launches a full-scale invasion of the Soviet Union	Japan attacks the US naval base at Pearl Harbor, bringing America into the war. In the following weeks it also attacks British territories in the Far East.

WRECKAGE OF X-7 MIDGET SUBMARINE

In September 1943, X-7 was one of three midget submarines sent to lay explosive charges beneath the German pocket battleship *Tirpitz* at her heavily protected anchorage in northern Norway.

X-7 was damaged during the attack and forced to the surface. Its commander, Godfrey Place, climbed up to signal surrender, but was forced overboard when the craft was engulfed with water and sank. Hours later one of the other three crewmen used an escape tank to make it back to the surface, but the remaining two were drowned.

IWM MAR 560

Godfrey Place was 22 years old when he commanded X-7 on its raid against the *Tirpitz*. He spent the rest of the war in a German prison camp and was awarded the Victoria Cross for his 'courage, endurance and utter contempt for danger'.

IWM A 21799

The midget submarine attack succeeded in putting the mighty *Tirpitz* out of action until April 1944. That November Lancaster bombers were sent to finish her off, destroying the ship with hits from two 'Tallboy' bombs (below).   IWM A 22633

The Germans raised the stern section of X-7 shortly after the attack on the *Tirpitz* but the remainder of the vessel was not recovered for another thirty years.

The bow and battery sections that you can see on display were raised to the surface by British divers in 1976.

Somewhere else in the same fjord lie the remains of X-5, one of the other submarines that took part in the operation. It is thought to have taken a direct hit from the *Tirpitz* with the loss of all four of its crew but its exact fate has never been established. It remains one of the unsolved mysteries of the Second World War.

BOMBERS

After the fall of France in the summer of 1940, the only way that Britain could strike back directly at Germany was from the air. But the Germans were ready for them; their anti-aircraft defences stretched from Paris to Denmark, made up of searchlights, guns like the **8.8cm Flak 36**, radar including the new **Würzburg A dish**, and night fighters like the **Messerschmitt Bf-110**. Such was the wall of fire that faced Allied aircrews as they ventured out on their exhausting nightly raids.

To make matters worse, even when the RAF's night bombers breached these defences, they did not at first have either the range or the accuracy to inflict serious strategic damage; many parts of Germany were out of reach and only one in four bombs fell within five miles of its target. The Allies were paying a high price for little strategic return.

Early in 1942, recognising the difficulty of hitting specific targets, the RAF began 'area bombing', subjecting wide areas of German cities to concentrated – and controversial – attack with high explosive and **fire bombs**. That same year the **Lancaster** and Halifax also entered service – heavy bombers with a much longer range.

From July 1942 the RAF was joined in the air war by the United States Army Air Force. The Americans flew daylight raids – their fighter planes equipped with **disposable petrol tanks** so that they could accompany the bombers all the way to the target area and back. The RAF continued to bomb at night. Under this combined assault the air war intensified but it was only from 1944 that the Allies eventually gained the upper hand – their new tactics and technology finally bearing fruit.

28

On the alert

German Würzburg A radar dishes like this one were used to locate hostile aircraft so that they could be targeted and stopped by guns and fighters. Here the usually circular dish is shown folded into its transit position.

IWM COM 559

DID YOU KNOW?

RAF aircrew were all volunteers, most aged in their late teens or early twenties. More than 55,000 of them were killed during the bomber offensive.

SPRING 1942	APRIL 1942	4–7 JUNE 1942	AUGUST 1942
Increasing merchant shipping losses to German U-boats put Britain's survival at stake	The Royal Air Force begins its systematic 'area bombing' of German cities	The US Navy gains a vital victory over the Japanese at the Battle of Midway, giving it naval superiority in the Pacific	After a stalled offensive in the Soviet Union in December 1941 and a renewed push in Spring 1942, the Germans reach the city of Stalingrad

SHIFTING SANDS

While the Royal Air Force waged its bombing campaign against Germany, the British Army was fighting the Italians and Germans in the deserts of North Africa. Success was vital. If the Suez Canal fell into enemy hands, Britain's trade and supply links to India and the East would be severed.

War in the featureless heat of the desert was very different; the humble **fuel can** and **water can** were as vital to a soldier as his gun, the **landmine** as important a form of defence as the **field gun**. It was man against man, and man against desert. And, from August 1942, it was Montgomery against Rommel – portrayed by the media as the most personal contest between military leaders in the war.

Bernard Law Montgomery and Erwin Rommel were charismatic, skilful commanders, respectful of each other and highly respected by their men. Both liked to stay close to the action. 'Monty' in particular making a point of being on the spot, flying the **Eighth Army flag** on his **Humber staff car**.

For three years, the desert war saw both sides fighting backwards and forwards across the same ground. The decisive moment came after the British repulsed a German attack in July 1942, and then launched one of their own at the same place in October. This was El Alamein and it proved to be a turning point for Britain in the war. As Prime Minister Winston Churchill put it: 'Before Alamein we never had a victory. After Alamein we never had a defeat.'

Montgomery knew it too, scooping up some sand from the battlefield to keep in a **glass jar**. Then it was time to fight onwards across the Mediterranean to Sicily and the Italian mainland, as the Allies clawed their way back to continental Europe.

Band of brothers
While under siege at Tobruk, defiant British troops decided to form a band. This improvised banjo, signed on the back by many of the men, was made from an aluminium bowl.
IWM EPH 9799

Danger sign
This yellow German flag was used to mark the boundary of a minefield. Both sides used mines to strengthen defensive positions.
IWM FLA 306

29

NOVEMBER 1942
Britain wins its first major land victory of the war at El Alamein (right). Fighting in North Africa continues until May 1943.
IWM E 18474

JANUARY 1943
A Soviet counter-offensive forces the Germans to surrender at Stalingrad. In July Germany is defeated at Kursk – its last offensive in the east.

SEPTEMBER 1943
After Allied landings in Sicily and on the Italian mainland, Italy surrenders to the Allies. The Germans continue to fight on Italian soil.

WASTELAND

On 22 June 1941, Germany launched an enormous invasion of the Soviet Union. The German Army was equipped for the kind of devastating and speedy victory that it had achieved against France, backed by thousands of **motorcycles**, tanks and aircraft. Ten days into the campaign, it had penetrated 500km into enemy territory and by December it was within sight of Moscow.

Then came winter, with temperatures plunging to -30°C – low enough to freeze the diesel fuelling the German advance. In the face of a Soviet fight-back, the Germans found themselves stuck in a prolonged campaign for which they were ill-prepared.

In the summer of 1942, they tried again, this time striking further south at Stalingrad, but they could not achieve a decisive breakthrough before the snows came once more. By this time, the power of the Soviet armaments industry was beginning to tell. Armed with weapons including the **PPSh 41** sub-machine gun and the **M1943 Goryunov SG-43** heavy machine gun, the Soviet troops had the advantage of stronger, more mobile firepower and from July 1943 onwards they began to push the German Army back.

Within two years, battle was raging in the streets of Berlin rather than Moscow, the once-proud **bronze eagles** of Hitler's Chancellery falling into the ruins of his Third Reich.

Cold comfort
When the war on the Eastern Front dragged on into a second winter, some German soldiers wore straw boots like these as insulation over their usual footwear.
IWM UNI 12917

OVERLORD

Not long after its evacuation at Dunkirk in 1940, the British Army began training for an invasion of the continental mainland. Four years later, on 6 June 1944 – D-Day – the assault, codenamed Overlord, was launched. An armada of ships had to cross the Channel to Normandy carrying a massive force of troops and equipment from Britain, Canada and America, while fighter planes and bombers offered protection and support from the skies.

General Montgomery summarised the plan in a **one-page outline**. The night before the attack, airborne troops would secure the edges of the landing sites, with equipment such as **foldable Welbike motorcycles** dropped alongside them to make them more mobile. Around dawn there would be a massive aerial and naval bombardment, and then a specially constructed fleet of **Landing Craft**

DID YOU KNOW?
The Allies could have been outnumbered 7 to 1 on D-Day. In the event, most of the 55 divisions that Germany had in France were caught away from Normandy – fooled by an elaborate Allied deception plan.

SPRING 1944
Japan invades India but by July is repelled by the British and Indian Armies (right)
IWM IB 291

6 JUNE 1944
The Allies land an invasion force in France. A week later, the Germans begin firing V1 flying bombs at Britain.

AUGUST 1944
The Red Army reaches the German border in the East. In September, US troops do the same in the West.

SIR PERCY HOBART: ENGINEER, VISIONARY, FUNNY MAN...

Launching an invasion from the sea called for specialist vehicles, and that was Percy 'Hobo' Hobart's area of expertise. In command of the 79th Armoured Division, he spent the eighteen months before D-Day developing a series of modified tanks, known collectively as his 'funnies'. They included the remarkable **Duplex Drive** that converted an ordinary Sherman tank into a propeller-driven amphibious vehicle.

Despite being decorated in the First World War, and enjoying a long military career, Hobart was forced into retirement in 1940 for being too much of a maverick. It took the intervention of Winston Churchill to make sure his unique talents did not go to waste, bringing him back into the army in 1941.

Master of invention

Sir Percy Hobart was responsible for the Sherman Crab tank (right) that flailed the beach with chains to destroy mines.

IWM H 20697, IWM MOD 950

would surge forward on to the beaches. The first wave included tanks, such as the **Sherman M4A4**, to pierce the German defences. Later, waves would carry the men and equipment needed to force a way through these holes and into the fields beyond.

Preparation was key; aerial photography was used to construct detailed **wood and plaster models** of the landing sites, so that every man could be given a thorough briefing on his route and objective; and every eventuality was considered, from **inflatable lifebelts** to **paper sickbags** and **portable communion sets**. It paid off; by nightfall on D-Day, Allied troops had established a firm foothold along a 50-mile stretch of the Normandy shoreline.

The Germans soon initiated an attack of their own, launching their first *Vergeltungswaffen* or 'revenge' weapons against south-east England. Together the **V1 flying bomb** and the **V2 rocket** brought terror to British civilians, but on the front line the Germans were on the retreat. By Autumn 1944, they had been pushed back over their own frontier by US troops in the West and by the Soviets in the East. By the following May, Berlin had fallen and defeat was inevitable. The war in Europe was over.

Tools of the trade

Naval surgeon Graham Airth carried his Royal Canadian Navy Medical Laboratory Box with him on D-Day as he attended to wounded soldiers being evacuated from the beaches.

IWM FEQ 889

DUST TO ASHES

Although the fighting in Europe came to an end in May 1945, it continued to rage on the other side of the world. In December 1941, Japan had attacked the United States and Britain's Asian colonies. By May 1942, it controlled much of Asia, including Burma, the Philippines and the Pacific.

The tide was turned at sea by the Battle of Midway, where the Japanese fleet was dealt a fatal blow by the Americans. It was a battle in which each side attacked the other's ships with aircraft launched from carriers – the Japanese bombers and **Mitsubishi Zero** fighters proving less successful than their US counterparts.

From that point on, US forces were able to advance island by island across the Pacific until they reached the Mariana Islands in 1944, which were close enough to the Japanese mainland to make raids by B-29 bombers possible. For the remainder of the war, the US Army Air Force subjected the cities and factories of Japan to devastating fire bomb raids, also dropping **aerial leaflets** urging civilians to move to the safety of the country.

In the face of these setbacks, the Japanese became increasingly desperate, their pilots sent out on 'kamikaze' missions to fly their planes deliberately into Allied ships. Some hit their target; others were shot down at the last minute. In both cases all that was left was the odd piece of debris – an **engine fragment** or a piece of fuselage.

Accepting defeat, it seemed, was not an option for the Japanese, but the dropping of atomic bombs on Hiroshima and Nagasaki in August 1945, coupled with a declaration of war by the Soviet Union, changed all that. Across Asia, Japanese officers arranged formal ceremonies of surrender with their enemies, marking the moment by handing over their **swords**. The Second World War was finally at an end.

DID YOU KNOW?

Japanese soldiers in remote locations refused to believe that their country had surrendered. A few remained hiding in the jungle for almost thirty years.

Peace at last

Many Japanese troops were unaware – or did not believe – that their country had surrendered. This sword was only handed over in Borneo on 31 October 1945, two months after the official end of the war.

IWM WEA 2272

DECEMBER 1944
The Germans fail in an offensive in the Ardennes, which became known as the Battle of the Bulge

30 APRIL 1945
Hitler commits suicide in Berlin, as Soviet troops storm his capital. On 8 May, the Allies declare Victory in Europe Day (left).
IWM HU41808

6 AUGUST 1945
The first atomic bomb is dropped on Hiroshima. Japan surrenders on 14 August 1945.

Laying down arms
Japanese officers line up to surrender their swords in Kuala Lumpur, Malaya 1945.
IWM IND 4845

OPENING IN 2021, IWM LONDON'S NEW
SECOND WORLD WAR GALLERIES

You are visiting IWM London at an exciting stage in its history. With the aim of bringing more of the museum's spaces into public use, and increasing the number of objects on display, an ambitious two-phase programme has been underway since 2012. Phase 1 was completed in 2014, with the opening of the new atrium and the award-winning First World War Galleries.

The second phase includes new Second World War Galleries and terrace displays, which will cover twice the area that we currently devote to this world-changing conflict. The displays will use objects, film, sound and other media to tell the stories of people across the globe whose lives were affected by this pivotal moment in modern history.

William Little, *Together*, 1941. IWM's traditional focus on Britain and the Commonwealth will be expanded to tell a bigger, global story.
IWM PST 4096

BEHIND THE SCENES

We're currently beavering away behind the scenes building the spaces, installing setworks, writing text, getting objects ready for display, and working with our designers to make sure everything looks just right. We've done all we can to reduce noise levels and building dust in the public spaces of the museum

A SNEAK PREVIEW

Here's a sneak preview of what to expect when the galleries are finished. Running from the mid-1930s to 1949, the story of the Second World War has been divided into six sections, each focused on answering a key question.

PEACE LOST: *Why was the peace of 1919 lost?*

The galleries begin with the political and economic tensions that overshadowed the world of the 1930s. The legacy of the First World War, combined with a major global financial crisis, created a world where governments everywhere came under pressure. Aggressive, autocratic regimes emerged in Germany, Italy and Japan, challenging the international *status quo*. The political decisions that these three nations took in the late 1930s slowly undermined the fragile peace that had existed for barely 20 years since the Armistice of 1918.

German Tail Fin
Tail fin from the Messerschmitt Me 110 flown by Heinz-Wolfgang Schnaufer, the Luftwaffe's highest-scoring fighter ace. It bears 121 'kill' markings.
IWM EPH 2961

Munich Agreement
British Prime Minister Neville Chamberlain makes a speech announcing 'Peace in our Time' at Heston Airport after meeting with Hitler in Munich, 30 September 1938.
IWM D 2239

WAR ENGULFS EUROPE:
Why did Total War spread across Europe?

The invasion of China by Japan in 1937 and the complete destruction of Poland by Germany and the Soviet Union in 1939 showed that the Second World War would be different in scale and impact from any conflict ever seen before. The galleries explore this Total War: indiscriminate, unrestrained, and physically, economically and morally challenging. In June 1940 Germany dramatically defeated France. Britain's war plans were shattered. Under threat of invasion and attacked from the air, Britain desperately had to work out how to survive. Only then could it start to fight back.

THE BATTLE FOR BRITAIN:
How did Britain survive in 1940?

From the summer of 1940 to the summer 1941, Britain and Germany emerged as the two main protagonists of the war in Europe. It was then that the war really started for the British people. With the shadow of a German invasion cast across the country, British towns and cities came under direct attack. First the Battle of Britain and then the Blitz placed Britain in the front line. As the galleries show, slowly Britain recovered, drawing on the strength of governments and servicemen exiled from Europe, and on the United States and people from across the Empire.

RAF Jacket
Ripped RAF jacket worn by Pilot Officer Frederick Harrold during the Battle of Britain, September 1940.
IWM UNI 13724

WORLD WAR: *Why did the war turn global?*

In June 1941 Germany attacked the Soviet Union. Overnight the scale and intensity of the war reached a new level. The German attack was the largest invasion the world had ever seen. The distances it covered were huge, the numbers involved were massive. Six months later Japan set aside its long-running war with China and boldly launched a rapid campaign to capture the European colonies of South-East Asia. At the same time Japan made a pre-emptive strike against the United States at Pearl Harbor, an act that brought America into the war in Europe as well as Asia. The conflict had now become a true world war.

Model Ship
Model of the SS *Llanstephen Castle* made by 13 year-old John Sadler, from the components of an aircraft kit with the addition of cotton rigging, during his evacuation to South Africa in August 1940.
IWM EPH_010895

VICTORY IN THE BALANCE:
Why did the Allies win and the Axis lose?

By mid-1942 the Axis powers of Germany, Italy and Japan had achieved widespread successes on the battlefield. They occupied large areas of the world and looked as if they might even win the war. But crucially they failed to work together, and lacked any coordinated strategy. By contrast, coming together in a strategic alliance under the leadership of the 'Big Three' of the Soviet Union, the United States and Great Britain, the Allies grew in strength year by year. On land, sea and air, in the east and in the west, step by step they hit back. Sharing their resources and dovetailing their plans, by 1945 they were in a winning position.

THE IMPACT OF TOTAL WAR:
What was the impact of Total War?

The consequences of global war were enormous both for nations and for individuals, as the galleries demonstrate. Although peace was re-established, conflict and confrontation continued. The new United Nations tried to bring those responsible for the war to account and to co-ordinate international reconstruction. But the world remained fragmented. As Britain struggled to hang on to its Empire, India was granted independence but broke up in a wave of violence into two new states, India and Pakistan. It was a time of turmoil and uncertainty, but one that looked forward with hope to the second half of the twentieth century.

Shadow of the bomb
The mushroom cloud from the atomic bomb dropped over Nagasaki on 9 August 1945, photographed from a B-29 bomber escorting the mission.
IWM MH 2629

PEACE AND SECURITY

Peace and Security: 1945 to 2014 uses clusters of objects to explore some key and often controversial episodes of recent history. Many of the objects are from the conflicts themselves. Others are made by artists to offer a different perspective. Together they raise questions about how and why we fight – and how we live with war and its unending aftermath.

Standing at the very heart of the museum, and confronting you as you enter this section is the **atomic bomb**. The death and devastation that this weapon unleashed on Hiroshima and Nagasaki in 1945 has cast a shadow over the world ever since, changing the way that war is fought, altering the balance of political power, and threatening the existence of all humanity. This is the troubled world explored in the rest of the displays.

DID YOU KNOW?

In 2014 a 13-year-old boy from Preston in Lancashire managed to achieve nuclear fusion in his school laboratory. In the 1950s scientists used the same process to create the hydrogen bomb – even more powerful than the atomic bomb.

Little Boy

This is one of five casings made for the 'Little Boy' atomic bomb between 1945 and 1950. Only one was ever used – for the bomb dropped on Hiroshima on 6 August 1945.

IWM MUN 3845 (lent by the US Government)

YOUR BRITAIN

Britain in 1945 was a country in transition. Men who had served in the nation's forces were issued with a set of clothes, such as a **demob suit** and a **trilby hat**, and allowed to return to civilian life. All around them there were signs of change: a new government intent on laying the foundations for the modern welfare state; prefabricated buildings to solve the housing shortage; and **posters** proclaiming the birth of a new, fairer, more caring Britain.

But the effects of war lingered on in everyday life – in the bombed-out buildings that littered the country's cities, in the continued rationing of food, fuel and furniture, and in the determined spirit of enterprise that saw bombsite debris given new life as a hobbyist's **train set** or a child's **scooter**.

Rebuilding Britain was an expensive undertaking, made all the more difficult by the need to maintain the country's position as a world power.

On 1 January 1949, wartime conscription was formally changed into National Service. This provided a steady stream of men to serve in Britain's Army as it attempted to police its global empire and fulfil its international responsibilities – from Palestine to Kenya, Egypt to Korea. And in the new atomic age, the investment required to make Britain a nuclear power put even further strain on the country's economy.

It would be some time before the British people could reap the benefits of the peace that they had fought so hard to secure.

Reminder of war
This American Willys MB Jeep was one of over 360,000 made between 1942 and 1945. Given to the British Red Cross Society in Italy by the commander of the US Fifth Army, it was brought back to Britain in 1947.
IWM 4007.50.2

PEACE AND SECURITY TIMELINE
In the decades since the Second World War, the military, political and social landscape of the world has changed – fuelled first by the ideological clash between communism and capitalism, and increasingly by fears of links between authoritarian regimes and terrorist organisations.

AUGUST 1947
Britain oversees the partition of its Indian Empire, creating the sovereign states of India and Pakistan

JUNE 1948
The Soviets block access to West Berlin to secure control of the entire city. The Western Allies fly in supplies eventually forcing the Soviets to back down.

Welcome home

David Harvey was given this scooter when he returned to London in 1945 after being evacuated during the Second World War. It is made from scraps of wood and metal recovered from the bomb-damaged Beehive Pub in Battersea, where he lived.

IWM EPH 10264

DID YOU KNOW?

Less than two months after leading his country to victory over Germany, Prime Minister Winston Churchill was voted out of office. He and his party were seen as the cause rather than the cure for Britain's social problems.

NEWS FROM ABROAD

During the Second World War, newsreels had brought images of distant lands, cities and people to British viewers, who were anxious to know how the conflict was progressing, and what their fighting men might be experiencing overseas. In the years afterwards, as the tumult of war subsided, the same places kept cropping up again on film, as the world — and Britain's place in it — began to change.

Before televisions became a fixture in British homes, these films reached viewers in the form of cinema newsreels, such as the 1946 **World Pictorial News**, which features a section on the emergence of a new post-war political order. Others were officially produced documentaries. There was the 1952 **Korean Carrier**, which followed the operations of British aircraft carriers HMS *Ocean* and HMS *Glory* during the Korean War. And there was **Operation Grapple**, produced by the Atomic Weapons Research Establishment in 1958 to show how Britain was developing its own arsenal of atomic weapons.

But the medium of film was also changing. Home movies provided a different perspective on events abroad, such as **Witness to the Partition of India** shot by Captain Clifford Williams in 1947 and **Hospital and Off Duty Scenes in Aden** filmed by Flight Officer Anne Peterkin.

OCTOBER 1949

Chinese Communists defeat the Chinese Nationalist Army and create a new communist state – the People's Republic of China

JUNE 1950

Communist North Korea invades UN-backed South Korea. War follows (right) until a ceasefire is agreed three years later.

IWM MH 33028

AUGUST 1961

East Germany's communist government builds the Berlin Wall to stop its citizens leaving the city for the West

WAR ON THE DOORSTEP

Over the past 40 years Britain has twice faced the challenge of political failure leading to armed conflict on the doorstep of its own communities.

In 1969 there came the disturbing sight of British troops patrolling streets in Northern Ireland. They remained there for some thirty years, struggling to keep order in the face of tension and violence between Catholic Republicans and Protestant Loyalists.

The troops themselves were often the target of violence, coming under fire from **assault rifles, pistols, grenade launchers** and bombs. It was an unfamiliar form of urban warfare that asked difficult questions of the soldiers — as you can hear in the exhibition's **recordings**.

The challenge that came on 2 April 1982 was dramatically different. When Argentinian forces invaded the distant Falkland Islands, few Britons even knew that they existed. But the British government under Prime Minister Margaret Thatcher had little hesitation in sending a task force 7,950 miles (12,800km) to the South Atlantic to drive them out.

On board a later British ship was artist Linda Kitson, commissioned by IWM to create an official artistic record. Her drawings — some completed at sea, others when she went ashore — show scenes from the war as it unfolded, capturing some of the energy and tension of a conflict that raged for 74 days until the Argentinians surrendered on 14 June.

LINDA KITSON: WAR ARTIST IN THE FALKLANDS

In 1982, 37-year-old Linda Kitson became the first woman to accompany British troops to the front line as a war artist. She specialised in **drawings** made with conté crayon, which meant she could capture a scene in a matter of minutes. It was an invaluable skill given the speed at which the troops moved across the islands and the freezing conditions in which she had to work with fingers exposed. She was well looked after by the soldiers. One even made her a camouflage armband to hold the five drawing tools she used most often.

Difficult sight

Kitson was overcome with emotion as she drew this image (right) of a burning *Sir Galahad*. She had come to know many of the 48 soldiers killed on board the ship.

MARY EVANS PICTURE LIBRARY/DAVID KIRBY, IWM ART 1553050

OCTOBER 1962

The US challenges the Soviet decision to site nuclear missiles in Cuba. The resulting crisis is the closest that the world has come to nuclear war.

AUGUST 1964

An attack on two of its ships escalates US involvement in a war between South Vietnam and the communist North. The war lasts until 1975.

APRIL 1969

British troops are sent to Northern Ireland (right) to stop Protestant attacks on Catholics. They are soon targeted by Republican terrorists.

IWM TR32956

MM38 EXOCET MISSILE

The Exocet missile gained notoriety during the Falklands Conflict when it was used by Argentinian forces against British ships.

A version launched from the air destroyed HMS *Sheffield* and the merchant ship *Atlantic Conveyor* in May 1982, and a shore-to-ship version like the one on display damaged HMS *Glamorgan* in June.

IWM MUN 3843

The missile used against HMS *Glamorgan* was designed to be fired from a ship but the Argentinians instead created an improvised shore-based launch trailer – possibly the one found abandoned (above) at Port Stanley when the Argentinians surrendered two days after the attack.

IWM FKD 2110

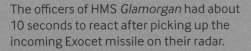

The officers of HMS *Glamorgan* had about 10 seconds to react after picking up the incoming Exocet missile on their radar.

The Navigating Officer executed a rapid turn away from the missile – preventing it from striking the ship's side and causing a potentially catastrophic explosion in the heart of the vessel.

Instead the missile skidded across the deck before it detonated, starting several fires and causing a fully fuelled and armed Wessex helicopter to explode.

Fourteen men were killed in the attack – but hundreds more might have died had it not been for the action taken during those vital ten seconds.

In an interview held in the IWM Sound Archive, Ian Inskip, an officer in HMS *Glamorgan*, remembers the burial service carried out at sea for the victims of the Exocet attack.

'We buried our dead at sunset. It was a beautiful evening. I remember the splash... splash...splash as the bodies were tipped over the side. It was very moving.

The position was marked on the chart and the relatives were eventually given a copy.'

'We buried our dead at sunset.'

QUEEN AND COUNTRY
Presented by the Art Fund

In 2003 Turner Prize-winning artist Steve McQueen was commissioned under the official war artists' programme at IWM to produce a new work about British forces serving in the Iraq War.

Inspired by the professionalism of the armed forces and the strength of community of the servicemen and women that he met, he came up with the idea of a set of postage stamps featuring the faces of those who had died. To exhibit the work, he created an oak cabinet, housing a set of sliding panels. Pull out a panel and you are presented with multiple identical images of a life lost — each image chosen by the soldier's family.

McQueen believes that the artwork will remain incomplete unless he can persuade the Royal Mail to circulate an official set of these stamps. That way, he says, 'it would form an intimate reflection of national loss that would involve the families of the dead and permeate the everyday — every household and every office'.

Faces of war

Each sheet of stamps is stored in the display cabinet according to the individual's date of death, which can be seen printed in the margin of the sheet.
IWM ART 17290

MAY 1972	**AUGUST 1974**	**JUNE 1979**	**DECEMBER 1979**
The US and Soviet Union sign the Strategic Arms Limitation Treaty (SALT I), limiting the number of nuclear warheads in their respective arsenals	Weeks after a Turkish invasion, the island of Cyprus is divided between Greece and Turkey along a 'Green Line' — a UN buffer zone	The two Cold War superpowers sign SALT II, placing a further limit on their nuclear weapons programmes	Soviet troops invade Afghanistan to install a pro-Moscow regime. Its forces remain in the country until 1989.

WAR THAT NEVER WAS

The USA and the Soviet Union were unlikely allies in the Second World War, united by the threat posed by Nazi Germany but divided by their vastly different political systems and ways of life. After the war, their mutual mistrust gradually escalated into a tense stand-off that became known as the Cold War. It was a war that people all over the world prayed would not ignite – for fear that the nuclear weapons developed by both countries would bring global annihilation.

The atomic bomb paved the way for a new generation of weaponry and military strategy. By the end of the 1950s warheads delivered by missile, such as **Blue Steel** or Polaris, were considered more accurate – and harder to defend against – than bombs dropped from aircraft. Strategic warheads intended to destroy cities, people and infrastructure were supplemented with 'tactical' weapons like the American **Lance** missile to be used against armies in the field. And both sides developed submarines that could serve as roaming, hidden missile launchers.

In fact, submarines became so important that a whole new range of defences had to be developed. **Sonobuoys** were dropped out at sea to detect submarine movement. Nuclear bombs like the British **WE. 177A** were adapted for use as anti-submarine depth charges. And the **Ikara rocket-powered glider** was designed for launch from a warship, capable of carrying a torpedo or nuclear bomb to a distant submarine's location.

None of these forms of attack and defence were ever used in anger. Instead, as the Soviet Union began to crumble at the end of the 1980s, and the Cold War came to an end, governments found that their stockpiles of weapons had become redundant. For almost fifty years, the world had lived in fear of a ruinous Third World War – the war that never was.

DID YOU KNOW?

Steve McQueen, the artist who created 'Queen and Country', is now a celebrated film director. His 2013 movie *12 Years a Slave* won three Academy Awards, including one for Best Picture.

Keys to power

These keys were used to activate a WE. 177 nuclear bomb before it was loaded on to its delivery aircraft. The WE. 177 was the last British bomb intended to be dropped from the air.

IWM MUN 4852

AUGUST 1980

Polish shipyard workers form a trade union and go on strike to defy the communist government – part of a wider bid for political freedom in Eastern Europe

APRIL 1982

Argentina invades the Falklands. Britain retakes the islands in June (left). The lives of 253 Britons and 655 Argentinians are lost.

IWM FKD 95

NOVEMBER 1983

US cruise and Pershing missiles arrive at bases in Europe, sparking fierce local protests. The missiles remain until 1991.

DRAWING THE LINE

War divides us, setting one side against another for reasons of nationality, ideology or faith. But sometimes peace requires its own form of division – in the drawing of lines and even the building of walls between opposing sides.

Nowhere was this more evident than in Germany after the Second World War, when the USA, Britain, France and Russia divided the country and its capital Berlin into four zones. The **wall** that was eventually built across the city became the most obvious example of the East-West ideological divide that characterised the Cold War.

Since the Second World War, most questions of war and peace have been dealt with by the United Nations. Sometimes this has meant bringing both sides to the negotiating table; other times putting troops on the ground to keep them apart – from **Korea** in the 1950s, to **Cyprus** in the 1970s and **Kosovo** in the 1990s. In all three cases, as in many others, UN troops remain in position to this day – policing the artificial dividing lines that make some sort of peace possible.

ALL CHANGED

In the days of the Cold War, some things felt certain. Superpower stood against superpower, ideology against ideology, missile against missile. But since the fall of the Berlin Wall in 1989, battle lines have become more blurred, enemies less easy to locate and threats less easy to predict.

The **mangled steels** of the World Trade Center are perhaps the most powerful reminder of the changed nature of warfare. The weapons used on 11 September 2001 were hijacked planes, the target the world's sole remaining superpower, the enemy a shadowy terrorist organisation called al-Qaeda.

America's response was to declare war – not on a country but on 'Terror' – and to fight for a victory that remains hard to define. With help from allies such as Britain, the US led an invasion of Afghanistan to overthrow the Taliban – the country's Islamic fundamentalist leaders – and hunt down the al-Qaeda terrorists believed to be based there.

Twelve years later British forces were still fighting in the country, pitting their far superior hardware, such as the **Harrier jet** and the remote-controlled **Desert Hawk drone**, against small groups of Taliban guerrilla fighters, with improvised roadside bombs, and extremists armed with a **suicide bomber's vest**.

City limit
Before the Berlin Wall was built, signs like this indicated the division between the British Sector of the city and East Berlin. Ignore such a sign and you risked being shot by an East German border guard.
IWM FEQ 863

NOVEMBER 1985
US President Ronald Reagan and Soviet leader Mikhail Gorbachev meet for the first time. At two later summits they agree to cut their nuclear arsenals.

DECEMBER 1988
A bomb explodes on board an American airliner over the town of Lockerbie in Scotland. Libyan terrorists are blamed.

NOVEMBER 1989
After communist regimes collapse in Poland and Hungary, citizens tear down the Berlin Wall, marking the symbolic end of the Cold War

JANUARY 1991
An international coalition goes to war to liberate Kuwait from its Iraqi invaders. The ground war lasts 100 hours and the Iraqis are expelled.

Testing times

A Russian-made Nuclear, Biological and Chemical Testing Kit found in Iraq in 1991. Saddam Hussein had openly used chemical and biological weapons against Iran and against Kurdish civilians in his own country.

IWM SUR 123

For six of those years British troops were also at war in Iraq. Prime Minister Tony Blair's decision to join the American-led invasion was controversial. The reasons given were clouded in uncertainty and changed as events unfolded: to destroy weapons of mass destruction if they were found; sever links that Iraqi leader Saddam Hussein might have with terrorists; and free the Iraqi people.

Hundreds of thousands took to the streets of London in 2003 to protest against the imminent invasion, with **posters** attacking the decision as the costly and complicated conflict progressed.

WITNESS STAND

In May 2000 two Libyans were put on trial for the bombing of an American airliner over Scotland twelve years earlier. Over the course of nine months, more than 200 people were called to the witness stand to give evidence, including policemen, a Libyan spy, CIA agents, explosives experts, arms dealers and baggage handlers. In January 2001, one of the accused was found guilty and sentenced to life in a Scottish prison. The other was found not guilty and allowed to go free.

The trial was steeped in controversy. Argument raged beforehand about how the case should be prosecuted – where, by whom and under what law? After all, the plane attacked was American, as were the majority of the 270 victims, but citizens of 20 other countries also died, including 11 residents of the small town of Lockerbie where the wreckage fell to the ground.

There was also the question of what constituted justice. Was it enough simply to establish the guilt or innocence of the two accused men? Or should the scope of the investigation be widened to discover whether they were acting under orders, who else was involved, and why the attack was carried out at all? These are questions that linger to this day – and which have gained more resonance in the light of later terrorist attacks such as in New York on 11 September 2001.

JUNE 1991
Following communism's collapse, politicians try to divide Yugoslavia into ethnically 'pure' states, sparking a bloody war in the region

SEPTEMBER 2001
Terrorists crash hijacked planes into the World Trade Center and the Pentagon. A month later the US leads an invasion of Afghanistan.

MARCH 2003
Coalition forces launch a controversial invasion of Iraq (left) and oust its leader Saddam Hussein

IWM OP-TELIC 03-010-20-067

THE HOLOCAUST EXHIBITION

Between 1933 and 1945, the Nazis and their collaborators persecuted and eventually murdered two thirds of Europe's Jews. The Holocaust Exhibition takes the visitor on a journey through this complex and challenging subject.

As you make your way through the exhibition you will get to view original artefacts, documents and film footage; you will discover how other groups including 'Gypsies' (Roma and Sinti), Poles, Soviet prisoners of war, Jehovah's Witnesses, homosexuals, the disabled and the mentally ill were also targeted; and you will hear 16 survivors of Nazi persecution tell their own stories.

This exhibition is not recommended for children under 14. Parents or carers wishing to take younger children into the exhibition are asked to keep them under close supervision at all times.

Culture under attack
A Berlin synagogue lies in ruins following the Nazi-instigated *Kristallnacht*, a pogrom against Jews in Germany and Austria on the night of 9–10 November 1938.

IWM FRA 204717

Symbol of oppression
The Nazis forced many Jews to wear a yellow star on their clothing. It marked them out for segregation, discrimination and – eventually, in most cases – for deportation to death camps in Nazi-occupied Poland. Stars of the type shown here were worn by Jews in Holland.

IWM INS 4350

HOLOCAUST TIMELINE
In the volatile years after the First World War, radical movements flourished on the left and right. Tapping into centuries of antisemitic prejudice, right-wing parties in Poland, Hungary, Romania and countries of the former Russian Empire launched violent attacks on Jews. The same would soon be true in Germany.

JANUARY 1933
Hitler becomes Chancellor of Germany. In April he orders a boycott of Jewish-owned businesses, strips Jews of citizenship and bars them from professions.

NOVEMBER 1938
The Nazis instigate a violent attack on synagogues and Jewish businesses. Around 90 Jews are murdered and some 30,000 taken to concentration camps.

UPPER FLOOR: RISE OF THE NAZIS

The exhibition opens with the rise to power of the Nazi Party and shows how, within months of Hitler becoming chancellor of Germany, Jewish people were made to feel unwelcome in a country where they had lived for centuries. A film explains how the Nazis took advantage of longstanding antisemitism in Europe to turn people against their Jewish neighbours.

A section called 'The Racial State' then shows how the Nazis saw the Germans as a 'Master Race' and wanted to cleanse the country of what they saw as 'alien' influences, including Jews, 'Gypsies' and so-called 'asocials'. You will learn how propaganda was used to spread this hatred, and how legislation was passed to set the German Jews apart from everyday society and deprive them of their livelihoods.

In 1939, shortly after the outbreak of the Second World War, the Nazis began a programme of extermination of people with mental illnesses and disabilities. German doctors and nurses took part in this shocking crime — a terrible indication of what would come under the cover of war, when six million of the nine million Jews living in Europe would be killed — one million of them children.

Parting gift
In 1938–1939, around 10,000 Jewish children were sent to Britain by parents desperate to protect them from the growing Nazi menace. One of them was Inge Pollak, who arrived from Austria in 1939 with this doll among her few personal possessions. It had been a birthday present from her mother, who later died in the camps.
IWM EPH 3922

14-year-old Jan Imich, photographed shortly after liberation in April 1945. Jan Imich had survived the notorious Mittelbau-Dora concentration camp.
© JAN IMICH

1939–1940		**JUNE 1941**	**JANUARY 1942**
Jews in occupied Poland are rounded up (right), stripped of property, forced to work and concentrated in ghettos IWM IA 37578		Germany invades the Soviet Union. SS murder squads shoot entire Jewish communities.	Nazi officials hold a conference in the Berlin suburb of Wannsee to discuss the implementation of the 'Final Solution'

GISELE FRIEDMANN: SURVIVOR

Gisele Friedmann was living in Paris when France fell to the Germans in 1940. She spent three years helping to keep other Jews in hiding until she was herself deported to Auschwitz-Birkenau in July 1943.

In January 1945, as the Nazis retreated, they tried to hide all evidence of their crimes at the death camp. Gisele and her fellow inmates were sent west, away from possible discovery. She spent five days travelling in a covered train, five more marching in freezing conditions, and then five more again travelling in an open truck before reaching Bergen-Belsen concentration camp.

Around 15,000 of the 66,000 prisoners who were sent on similar death marches did not survive. Some died of starvation, disease and exposure; others were shot for being too weak or ill to continue.

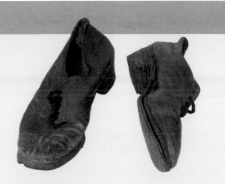

Death march shoes

These were the shoes that Gisele Friedmann was wearing when she was liberated from Bergen-Belsen in April 1945. The possession of these sturdy shoes saved her life.
IWM EPH 7050

LOWER FLOOR: THE HOLOCAUST

Within weeks of war breaking out, German forces overran Poland and imposed a brutal regime. They singled out the Jewish population for especially vicious treatment, forcing them to work and rounding them up into overcrowded ghettos. Half a million Jews died in these places from starvation and disease.

Then came the German invasion of the Soviet Union in June 1941. Three million Soviet prisoners of war were taken in the first eight months, held captive in open pens where thousands died of exposure and starvation. Behind the lines, SS murder squads known as *Einsatzgruppen* ('Action Groups') began rounding up and shooting Jews and Communists. Nearly one and a half million Jews are estimated to have been killed in this way.

By 1942, the Nazis had adapted their methods to devise what they called the 'Final Solution' to the Jewish question in Europe. Finding shooting to be too distressing for the soldiers involved, they introduced a more efficient killing process: Jews across Europe were rounded up, forced on to trains and transported to specially constructed 'death camps'.

As trains arrived at Auschwitz-Birkenau, the largest of the camps, Jewish families were forced into a process of selection. About one in five was picked out by an SS doctor for slave labour; the rest were killed immediately in gas chambers.

This was the horror that confronted the world when the Allies finally reached the death camps — though the facts of the Nazi persecution programme had actually been known for over three years.

MARCH 1942	**1941–1944**	**JANUARY 1945**	**APRIL 1945**
The Nazis begin moving people out of the ghettos for 'Resettlement in the East' – a euphemism for their deportation to death camps	Millions of Jews are murdered in the gas chambers of Chelmno, Belzec, Sobibor, Treblinka, Majdanek and Auschwitz-Birkenau	The retreating Nazis force their prisoners to march to camps inside the Reich. Thousands more die.	Western Allied troops begin to discover the concentration camps. The graphic reports and film of what they find there horrify the world.

THE LORD ASHCROFT GALLERY

The Lord Ashcroft Gallery: Extraordinary Heroes **tells the stories of over 250 remarkable people. All of them faced adversity and all were awarded either the Victoria Cross (VC) or the George Cross (GC) – the highest recognitions of bravery that can be given by Britain and, for many years, the Commonwealth.**

Every story told in the gallery – funded by a £5 million donation from Lord Ashcroft KCMG PC – involves an act of great bravery. However, by comparing the descriptions given in the official award citations, it is possible to identify similarities between stories. The gallery therefore uses seven 'qualities of bravery' to group the medals: boldness, aggression, leadership, skill, sacrifice, initiative and endurance.

But, taken as a whole, the many extraordinary stories told in the exhibition can also help us to answer one fundamental question: what is bravery?

DID YOU KNOW?

Two 15-year-olds have been awarded the Victoria Cross – one in 1857, the other in 1860.

Heroes all

Top row (from left): Israel Harding VC, Abdul Hafiz VC, Odette Sansom GC; Middle row (from left): George Dorrell VC, James Magennis VC, John Quinton GC; Bottom row (from left): Edward Bradbury VC, Manley James VC, David Nelson VC.

IWM Q 80536; IWM IND 3508; IWM HU 3213; IWM Q 79792; IWM A 26940A; IWM HU 3161; IWM VC 115; IWM VC 631; IWM Q 80586

Victoria Cross

The Victoria Cross is awarded to recognise acts of great courage in the heat of battle under enemy fire.

IWM HU 69722

George Cross

The George Cross is given for acts of gallantry carried out in peacetime, or in war but away from the intensity of battle.

IWM OMD 5297

BOLDNESS

Sometimes bravery is about dash, daring and quick thinking. **Israel Harding VC** exhibited just such qualities when an unexploded 10in shell pierced HMS *Alexandra* off the coast of Egypt in 1882. Assessing the situation in a flash, he threw water over the shell to cool it down, then grabbed it and submerged it in a bucket. The shell had landed near the ship's gunpowder magazine and, had it burst, would have caused many fatalities.

AGGRESSION

There are times in the uproar of battle when you need to rely on speed and sheer force to carry the day. Such was the case with **Abdul Hafiz VC** on 6 April 1944 when he led his men against a well-defended Japanese position in India. Dashing up an exposed slope, and suffering wounds to his leg, Hafiz grabbed the barrel of an enemy machine gun before it could do any more damage, and kept advancing while firing from the hip with a Bren gun. The Japanese were put to flight, but Hafiz was killed as he pursued them down the other side of the hill.

Last gun standing

The gun manned by Edward Bradbury VC, George Dorrell VC and David Nelson VC was salvaged after the battle. It is on display in the First World War Galleries on Level 0.

IWM ORD 102

LEADERSHIP

It takes a certain type of bravery to take command of a difficult situation and inspire belief, hope and confidence in your comrades. **Manley James VC** displayed it in March 1918 in the face of the Germans' massive Spring Offensive.

James led his company forward to meet the Germans, capturing 27 prisoners and two machine guns. Ignoring a wound, he stayed to see off three further German attacks, and then refused to retreat when they finally broke through. Instead he led a counterattack to buy the rest of the battalion time to withdraw, and then told his men to run for it while he worked a machine gun alone. James was eventually taken prisoner but not before he had saved the entire battalion from being cut off.

DID YOU KNOW?

Captain Charles Upham of New Zealand is the only combat soldier to have been awarded the Victoria Cross twice — in Crete in 1941 and Egypt in 1942.

SKILL

Bravery is about keeping your head under pressure. That doesn't just mean staying calm but having the presence of mind to act appropriately — harnessing your skill, resources and technical knowledge to greatest effect.

Such was the type of bravery exhibited by **Edward Bradbury VC**, **George Dorrell VC** and **David Nelson VC** of L Battery, Royal Horse Artillery, when they came under surprise attack from the Germans in 1914. It was soon a case of one British gun firing against twelve German ones, but despite terrible injuries — and the death of Bradbury — the men of L Battery kept firing. Two and a half hours later they stopped, just as reinforcements arrived to drive the Germans away and capture eight of their guns.

JOHNSON BEHARRY: SOLDIER, DRIVER, HERO...

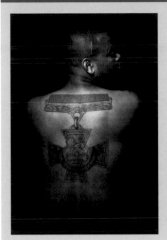

In April 2005, Johnson Beharry became the first recipient of the Victoria Cross since 1982 – and only the twelfth since the end of the Second World War. His citation refers to not one but two acts of extreme bravery performed some six weeks apart during his deployment in Iraq in 2004.

In both cases, Beharry was driving a Warrior Armoured Fighting Vehicle when it came under ambush. Under intense fire and at great personal risk to himself, he managed to get his fellow crewmen to safety despite, on the second occasion, sustaining a serious head injury for which he had to undergo brain surgery. He was still recovering when he heard about his award. 'I was speechless,' he said. 'Maybe I was brave, I don't know. I think anyone else could do the same thing.'

Body on the line
A portrait of Johnson Beharry taken for IWM by acclaimed war photographer Don McCullin.
PORTRAIT BY DON MCCULLIN FOR THE IMPERIAL WAR MUSEUM

SACRIFICE

What could be braver than to offer up your life to save another? That's the sacrifice that **John Quinton GC** made in 1951 when the Wellington aircraft in which he was training broke apart after a mid-air collision. Quinton and a 16-year-old cadet found themselves in the severed rear compartment of the plane with only one parachute. Quinton clipped it to the cadet, showed him the rip-cord and told him to jump. The boy survived. Quinton did not.

ENDURANCE

It's one thing to be brave on the spur of the moment, but quite another to sustain your courage in full knowledge of the price you might have to pay. That was the type of bravery required of **Odette Sansom GC** as a Special Operations Executive agent in occupied France in the Second World War — and even more so after she was captured, tortured and sent to Ravensbrück concentration camp. She refused to give away the hiding place of other British agents and defied her captors to survive the war.

INITIATIVE

Sometimes bravery isn't just about following orders, it's about seeing what needs to be done and doing it. On the night of 11–12 June 1982, **Ian McKay VC** was faced with just such a situation. His platoon commander had been wounded in an advance that had been stopped by Argentinian machine gun fire. Acting on his own initiative, McKay led a four-man assault on the machine gun bunker. He threw in a grenade but was killed just before the bunker was silenced. The British advance continued.

Highly decorated
Odette Sansom's medals, with the George Cross on the far left.
IWM OMD 3945

ART

Throughout the museum, you will find regularly changing art and photography displays — drawing on IWM's vast art collections and the many new works that IWM continues to commission or acquire.

IWM holds the most important and extensive collection of British war art in the world. When the museum was first established in 1917, it immediately began to commission artists in the field, and would later acquire other official works commissioned by the British government.

By 1920, when the museum first opened, it could already call on a collection of over 3,000 artworks, including images by celebrated artists such as John Singer Sargent, Paul and John Nash, Percy Wyndham Lewis and Christopher Nevinson.

DID YOU KNOW?

There are over 85,000 items in the museum's art collections. If you only spent five minutes looking at each one, it would take you almost ten months to view them all.

A scene of life and death

Detail from *Spring in the Trenches, Ridge Wood, 1917* by Paul Nash. Commissioned by the Ministry of Information in 1919, the painting is an attempt to capture the optimism Nash felt when he first encountered the Western Front as a soldier in spring 1917 — a sense that nature could prevail over man's destruction.

IWM ART 1154

Tools of war

These paint brushes were used by John Nash. They can be seen on display in the First World War Galleries.

IWM EPH 9007

SIR MUIRHEAD BONE: FIRST OFFICIAL WAR ARTIST

Muirhead Bone specialised in small, detailed, black and white drawings – exactly the type of image that could be created quickly at the front and reproduced well in the printed propaganda of the Department of Information. An established member of the London art scene, he was 40 years old when he became Britain's first official war artist in July 1916.

Bone went on to play a key role in the establishment of IWM towards the end of the war and earned a knighthood in 1937. When war broke out again in 1939, he sat on the newly-formed War Artists' Advisory Committee, and also produced officially commissioned works of his own.

Art of war
Muirhead Bone makes a sketch behind the Allied lines at the Somme. In his first six week period in the field he completed 150 drawings.   IWM Q 3111

A NEW WAR

At the outbreak of the Second World War, the Ministry of Information set up the War Artists' Advisory Committee to oversee its official war art programme. Over half of the 6,000 works produced by the programme are now in the museum's keeping – including pieces by Henry Moore, Graham Sutherland, John Piper and Stanley Spencer.

From the outset the scheme embraced a wide range of artists and styles, and from 1942 it extended its scope to include theatres of war in North Africa and the Far East. Some 400 artists took part – and three died in the course of their work: Eric Ravilious, Albert Richards and Thomas Hennell.

Mounting a defence
A Balloon Site, Coventry by Laura Knight. The ballet and the circus were frequent subjects of Knight's paintings and it is the coordinated physical performance skills of the barrage balloon team that she emphasises here.
IWM ART LD 2750

Portrait of an aircraft carrier
HMS Glorious in the Arctic by Eric Ravilious, one of the first artists signed up by the War Artists' Advisory Committee. Ravilious went missing in action in September 1942.
IWM ART LD 283

Human cost

Sectarian Armour — a steel jacket created by Belfast-born artist John Kindness in response to the troubles in Northern Ireland. The front of the jacket, which can be seen on **Level 2**, is adorned on the left with symbols of those loyal to Britain (the Queen and the bulldog) and on the right with Irish Republican iconography (the Virgin Mary, and an Ulster hog). On the back of the suit a Republican funeral is joined to a Loyalist one by a single seam — highlighting the absurdity of the divisions that serve to unite the communities only in grief.

JOHN KINDNESS
SECTARIAN ARMOUR, 1994
IWM ART 16636
©THE ARTIST

Putting work first

A note written by official war artist Linda Kitson while recording the Falklands Conflict in 1982. Several of Kitson's drawings are displayed in **Peace and Security** on **Level 2**.

IWM ART 15530 63

59

CONTEMPORARY VIEW

Today the museum continues to acquire new works and to commission thought-provoking perspectives on war, including the conflicts in Northern Ireland, the Falklands, Bosnia, Iraq and Afghanistan. Some of these works form part of the **Peace and Security** displays on **Level 2**. These include *Two Blue Car Doors*, a reflection on the troubles in Northern Ireland by sculptor Bill Woodrow, and Bruce McLean's *Broadside*, a powerful riposte to the media frenzy surrounding the Falklands Conflict.

EXPLORE FURTHER AND GET INVOLVED

The exhibits in the museum are only a fraction of the collections held by IWM. If you would like to find out more about any aspect of twentieth and twenty-first century conflict, there is no better place to start than by exploring our online collections database, which you can access at **iwm.org.uk/collections.**

ART

Our art collection is discussed in detail on pages 56–59. We also have a separate collection of almost 20,000 international war posters and the War Artists' Archive, which includes papers relating to the works produced under the war art schemes.

BOOKS & PUBLICATIONS

We maintain a national reference library of books, pamphlets and periodicals including unit histories, technical manuals, biographies, autobiographies and other publications on the military, economic, social and cultural aspects of war since 1914.

DOCUMENTS

We are privileged to hold the private papers of almost 20,000 men, women and children who have experienced warfare. We also have an extensive collection of captured German records dating from the period of the Third Reich as well as official documents concerning the war crimes trials held in Nuremberg and Tokyo after the Second World War.

Menu / Search

COLLECTIONS ONLINE

SEARCH OUR COLLECTIONS

Explore around 800,000 items that tell the story of modern war and conflict, collected by the museum since 1917.

Search

EXHIBITS

The museum contains all kinds of objects: uniforms, flags, badges and insignia; medals and decorations; military equipment; weapons and ammunition; vehicles, aircraft and ships; mementoes and a huge miscellany of personal possessions, both everyday and unusual. We have tens of thousands of other objects in our care, many of which can now be searched for online.

FILM

We hold over 23,000 hours of moving images, dating from the First World War through to recent conflicts in Iraq and Afghanistan. A great deal of the footage – most of it official but some amateur – can be viewed online, providing an extraordinary breadth and depth of military, political, social and cultural history.

Breadth of interest
Poster issued during the Second World War by the
Ministry of Supply; a photograph of British forces
waiting to board a Chinook helicopter in Afghanistan,
2006; a nurse's diary from the First World War.
IWM PST 14894, IWM HTF-2006-043-427, DOCUMENTS.1269

SOUND

Search our collections online where you can also
listen to veterans and non-combatants talking
about their experiences during the First and Second
World Wars and in conflicts up to the present day.
It is the largest oral history archive of its kind in the
world. We also hold a substantial amount of BBC
broadcast material from the Second World War as
well as music and sound effects.

PHOTOGRAPHY

IWM has long been the custodian of all official
photographs taken by the armed forces as well as
other government departments such as the former
Ministry of Information. Add in all the images taken
by other photographers – professional and amateur
– and our collection amounts to several million
photographs, covering all aspects of conflict from
the Crimean War to the present day.

Civilians in war
Interior of a hospital train, with nurses from a
London hospital in attendance. Second World War
Press Agency photographer.
IWM HU 82704

IWM LONDON & YOU

OPENING HOURS

Open daily from 10am–6pm
Closed 24, 25, 26 December

Research Room (by appointment only)
Mon–Thurs (closed on Fridays and Bank Holidays)
Morning session 10am–1pm
Afternoon session 2pm–5pm
iwm.org.uk/research/research-facilities

Admission Free
There may be a charge for exhibitions

GENERAL ENQUIRIES AND INFORMATION

Enquiries **020 7416 5000**
iwm.org.uk/contact-us

IWM London
Lambeth Road
London SE1 6HZ

iwm.org.uk

FAMILY ACTIVITIES, SCHOOLS AND LEARNING

We offer a wide range of activities and resources for schools, families and the general public. These include interactive sessions, performances, talks, workshops, conferences and online resources. Visit **iwm.org.uk/visits/iwm-north/groups** and **iwm.org.uk/whats-on**

GROUP BOOKINGS

Groups do not need to book in advance for a general visit. Groups of ten or more qualify for a discounted rate for our special ticketed exhibitions. To find out more, visit **iwm.org.uk/visits/iwm-london/ groups**. Groups catering packages are available in the café. Email **events@iwm.org.uk** for more details.

FACILITIES FOR DISABLED VISITORS

All areas of the museum are accessible to wheelchairs. Telephone **020 7416 5000** or visit **iwm.org.uk/visits/iwm-london/access**

SHOPPING

Visitors to the museum Shop can enjoy browsing our extensive range including books, DVDs and CDs, prints and postcards, educational resources, and a large selection of gifts and souvenirs for all ages. You can also buy directly from our Online Shop via a terminal within our stores and have items sent straight to your home. Our Online Shop can be found at **iwmshop.org.uk**

IWM PST 13959   IWM PST 3645

CAFÉ

The Café, situated on **Level 0**, is a great place to relax. It has a terrace overlooking the park and is open from 10am to 5.30pm. It offers an excellent range of food cooked on the premises, using fresh and seasonal ingredients.

MEMBERSHIP

Joining us as a member is a great way to support our work. Benefits include free entry to all our branches (HMS *Belfast*, Churchill War Rooms and IWM Duxford all charge a general admission fee), and discounts in IWM restaurants, cafés and shops. As a charity we depend on our members' support to enable the stories of those impacted by conflict to continue to be told from one generation to the next, and to ensure that our world-leading collection and historically important sites are protected for the future.

For full details on how you can become a member and make a difference, please speak to a member of staff or a volunteer, or visit **iwm.org.uk/membership**

KEEP IN TOUCH

If you would like to hear about future events and exhibitions, sign up at **iwm.org.uk/enews/ signup** to receive our eNews. You can also connect with us on Twitter, Instagram and Facebook.

MEETINGS AND EVENTS

The Atrium, a Roof Terrace, and a range of meeting/ conference rooms are available for corporate or private events. To make an enquiry please email **events@iwm.org.uk** or call **020 7091 3140**.

VOLUNTEERING

We are privileged to have volunteers support IWM in a variety of roles and we value their expertise, knowledge and dedication. Are you ready to be a part of our story?

To find out more, and to search and apply for volunteer vacancies, please visit **iwm.org.uk/volunteer**

IWM PRINTS

IWM is pleased to offer high quality prints and canvases from our unique collections. Choose from a wide selection of paintings, drawings and posters. Prints are available in a range of sizes and frames, and are delivered to your door. Place your order from one of our in-store terminals or online at **iwmprints.org.uk**

IWM is a charity and all profit from sales of these products supports the work of the museum.

SUPPORT US

IWM is a charity and we depend on supporters like you. Help us to care for and display our exceptional Collections, and to inspire visitors of all ages to build an understanding of war and conflict and how these events shape our world.

All donations will be a valuable contribution in helping us to continue our work. If you would like to support us, please contact the Development Department. Telephone **020 7091 3042** or email **iwmdevelopment@iwm.org.uk**, or to make a donation online visit **iwm.org.uk/support-us**

ABOUT IWM

IWM is a global authority on conflict and its impact in Britain, its former Empire and Commonwealth, from the First World War to the present day and beyond. We collect objects and stories that give an insight into people's experiences of war and we preserve them for future generations. By telling these stories on our website – **iwm.org.uk** – and across our five branches, we aim to help people understand why we go to war and the effect that conflict has on people's lives. As a charity, we rely on admission fees, our cafés, sales in our shops (including **iwmshop.org.uk**) and donations to continue our work and to ensure that the stories of those who have lived, fought and died in conflicts since 1914 continue to be heard.

IWM NORTH

The multi-award-winning **IWM North** was designed by world-renowned architect Daniel Libeskind to represent a globe shattered by conflict. The iconic building houses innovative and dynamic exhibitions, including hourly digital media Big Picture Shows, designed to explore how war shapes lives. There is also a changing temporary exhibition programme as well as regular public events all aimed at inspiring knowledge and encouraging debate.

The Quays, Trafford Wharf Road, Manchester M17 1TZ.

IWM DUXFORD

Set within the best-preserved Second World War airfield in Europe, **IWM Duxford** is a vibrant museum that marries its fascinating past with award-winning interactive exhibitions, working hangars and an exciting programme of events. Home to an impressive collection of over 200 aircraft as well as tanks, military vehicles and boats, discover the fascinating stories behind the machines that changed our lives forever and the impact they had on the development of future technology.

Cambridgeshire, CB22 4QR.

CHURCHILL WAR ROOMS

Inside **Churchill War Rooms** lie the original Cabinet War Rooms – the secret underground bunker which sheltered Churchill and his staff during the Second World War. Explore the historic rooms, including the Map Room where the books and charts are exactly where they were left when the door was locked in 1945. Discover the stories of those who worked underground as London was bombed above them, and explore the life and legacy of Winston Churchill in the Churchill Museum.

Clive Steps, King Charles Street, London SW1A 2AQ.

HMS BELFAST

HMS *Belfast* is the most significant surviving Second World War Royal Navy warship, with a history that extends to the Cold War, Korea and beyond. Once home to a crew of up to 950 men, HMS *Belfast* tells the stories of those who lived on board this warship. Explore nine decks of seafaring history including the machines in the Engine Room that powered her across the world. Hear the sailors' battle stories and take control of a fleet in the Operations Room.

The Queen's Walk, London SE1 2JH.

For information relating to all IWM branches, please call **020 7416 5000**, or go to the website: **iwm.org.uk**